# Rising Stars 2014

I0392576

*Rising Stars 2014* is organised by New Ashgate Gallery and supported by Arts Council England and Billmeir Charitable Trust. We work in partnership with Milton Keynes Arts Centre, Smiths Row, University for the Creative Arts and a-n The Artists Information Company.

**8 March - 19 April 2014**
**New Ashgate Gallery**
Waggon Yard
Farnham
Surrey GU9 7PS

newashgate.org.uk
gallery@newashgate.org.uk
01252 713208

**26 April - 31 May 2014**
**Milton Keynes Arts Centre**
Parklands
Great Linford
Milton Keynes MK14 5DZ

miltonkeynesartscentre.org
info@miltonkeynesartscentre.org
01908 608108

**7 June - 12 July 2014**
**Smiths Row**
The Market Cross, Cornhill
Bury St Edmunds
Suffolk IP33 1BT

smithsrow.org
enquiries@smithsrow.org
01284 762081

Editor: Outi Remes
Copyright: New Ashgate Gallery
Design: hkgraphics.co.uk
Published by Lulu 2014
ISBN: 978-1-291-74606-8

# Contents

# Rising Stars 2014:
## fresh talent and ideas for the UK's crafts

*Rising Stars 2014* is a platform to view and collect some of the most exciting new crafts by emerging makers from crafts and applied arts programmes across the UK. This curated, selling exhibition will tour from New Ashgate, Farnham, to Milton Keynes Arts Centre and Smiths Row, Bury St Edmunds. *Rising Stars* exhibition enables new makers to access the market place and collectors during these challenging economic times. The artwork in the exhibition is available for sale and every sale supports the maker.

The makers were selected following an open call for application with a strong response. The selection panel consisted of Dr Maureen Bampton, Bluecoat Display Centre, Liverpool, Rebecca Skeels, University for the Creative Arts, Farnham and Lucy Day, Day + Gluckman curatorial partnership and a professional development advisor at a-n. Opportunities such as *Rising Stars* are needed more than ever, as arts funding is being reduced and some art organisations focus on established names that are less risky than presenting new makers or students.

The winner of the *Rising Stars 2014* Professional Development Award will be announced in the *Rising Stars* private view on 7 March. The exhibition has a related professional development programme that supports emerging makers. This includes a symposium, talks and AIRTIME events with craft leaders from organisations such as Crafts Council, a-n The Artists Information Company and Surrey Arts, supporting artists' skills development.

*Rising Stars 2014* is produced by New Ashgate Gallery in partnership with Milton Keynes Arts Centre and Smiths Row is supported by Arts Council England and the Billmeir Charitable Trust. New Ashgate Gallery would also like to thank the University for the Creative Arts and a-n The Artists Information Company for their support.

**Dr Outi Remes**
Gallery Director, New Ashgate Gallery

# Star Gazing

The path to success, commercial or otherwise, is invariably a rocky one and so it is always with genuine admiration and humility that I sit down with fellow selectors of an open exhibition to make decisions about who goes through and who will not. It is also with genuine curiosity, current and recent graduates are reflectors of wider concerns, not only within their own fields of arts and design, but also in society and amongst them could be a few who will change the course of how we think about art, craft, function and aesthetics. *Rising Stars* is a therefore a wonderful opportunity for makers, judges and hosts alike to be part of this mapping process and contribute to the wider dialogue around the role of the creative arts in this country.

As a curator I bring a certain set of prejudices to the table and these inform the choices that I make. Whether in the flesh or digitally an artwork, product or object needs to intrigue me. I want to want to know more. It may well be that the process is one that I have not encountered before: the patina and fabrication may have come about through time-honoured means and yet somehow the maker has found a way for it to have a new conversation. The crafting of an exquisite work never fails to ignite my attention – I love envisioning the process of making and having the tactile evidence in front of me:  the rough and the smooth, the coloured and the minimal. All have a part to play in that most early of senses - delight and wonder. But also the object needs to work, to function as intended. Is it to be shown in a gallery? In a cabinet? How will it fare with and without other works around it? If the work is to be used: to be drunk from, to sit on… has the balance between the aesthetic and the intent been found? And those delicious things in between – the works that are neither art nor craft but glide seamlessly between the two – daring us to use them, or to covet and revere them.  My colleague Eliza was recently given an 18th century chinoiserie tea cup, probably one of a now long lost set, still beautiful, aged and worn. The temptation would be to house it somewhere safe, to forbid the children from touching and revelling in its design. Instead it has pride of place amongst her coffee cups, and is used frequently and with pleasure as part of a familiar 21st century morning ritual.

And so, from *Rising Stars 2014*, which pieces will survive the iniquities of judgement and then of time? With some pieces I start to imagine personal narratives, imbuing works with additional significance. Being selected is but one part of their journey.  Others will be picked up (we hope!) by manufacturers and will become familiar household entities. Still more will serve as seed ideas for their makers who, encouraged by their success, will gain the confidence and exposure to keep making, keep creating. For those makers who did not make it through this time? Hopefully they will be spurred to try again… this is after all but one of many, many opportunities along the way.

When work moves from the studio to the outside world it takes on a new direction, and the maker is the most important conduit in that process. How you choose to present your work is key to ensuring it has the best chance. Whilst a judge's preference would be to see all applications in the flesh logistically this is not always possible. In addition so much work is now seen via the internet it is ever more important to ensure that you have good documentation of your work. A good photograph will reveal more of the work than you perhaps imagined. A bad photograph is just that, and does neither maker nor photographer any favours. But in this case I would also include that, unlike a fashion or interiors spread (where tantalising hints of your jewellery, or cup, or spoon are shown alongside equally desirable competitors) the viewer needs to get a clear sense of each facet of the work. I want to see a beautiful/intricate/complex/feisty (delete as appropriate) bracelet rather than a well-turned wrist. And human beings like to pick things up, to touch and feel the material (witness a group of five year olds in a museum…or equally most visitors to a gallery or shop). Technology is still some way off allowing us that experience online – so how can you convey the lustre or texture of your work? Small details alongside wider shots can play a huge part in allowing a viewer to get a better sense of what it is that they are looking at. Admittedly it can also reveal the flaws, but unless these are intentional they should not perhaps be there. Quite literally putting your work in the spotlight can be a great way of assessing it and editing back to the pieces that you are most happy with. Let good lighting and an appropriate setting ply their magic. Ultimately, creating context for how and where you envisage your work ending up helps us, the audience and potential commissioner or buyer make decisions about what we are looking at.

Displaying any kind of work, be it visual art, design or applied arts, needs a subtle approach. Deciding how to place works in relation to each other is a complex process – think of a window display that makes you stop and feast on the contents compared to the one you walk past day in day out and barely notice what is there. An exhibition, be it of your own work in a cabinet, or in a gallery space, set against or with other people's should consider the following: do the works complement or challenge one another? Is there enough room around the works to allow them space to breathe? Equally an intimate work can be enhanced by a small, discreet space that encourages the viewer to look harder. The platform that works sit on can radically alter how we perceive them. Laura White's work continually questions notions of display and taste and her plinths are often integral to the work: designed and built with each artwork in mind. For a recent solo exhibition at SPACEX in Exeter each plinth was specifically made for the individual sculptures that are homed by them. Height and style being determined by the artwork itself. In Meekyoung Shin's Translation series (exquisite copies of Asian ceramics, translated into soap) the transient nature of culture and trade is emphasised by using packing cases as plinths. Framing can likewise provide focus to works, quite literally setting boundaries to the work. On the other hand framing can also kill a work flat by being too dominant. It is a delicate but important balance to strike. Creating aesthetic harmonies between works is incredibly satisfying. Equally setting up juxtapositions of different works can often provide a new context for the art on display. By exaggerating difference the key factors determining the piece can come to the fore: the materials, colours, texture, function. Overall the work itself needs to shine through, enhanced rather than overawed by its surroundings and fellows.

Exhibiting work comes in many forms and with the omnipotent presence of the web at our disposal artists in all disciplines should be prepared to make full use of it. Understanding who your audience is and who you might want it to be is an important factor when deciding how best to present your work online. From sites, to blogs, Facebook, Twitter, Pinterest and the multitude of others out there the key is to ensure that one dovetails into another, in essence you are creating a brand for your work. A consistent detail, a motif image perhaps, running through each piece of marketing or publicity material over a set period can help create a unique identity and gain you followers, who will ideally turn into buyers and commissioners. This can be updated each time a new series or strand comes to fruition. Identifying where your work might realistically sit in the sprawling framework of the market is an evolving process but you will naturally gravitate to platforms that you find of interest, and you need to exploit the opportunities that you find there. Artists are always advised to key into a limited number of galleries, locally and nationally, who tend to show work that will empathise with their own. The maker market is no different; in fact it is probably broader. Doing your research may take time but the benefits reaped are really worth it. A point to note however is that good gallerists and agents will show a spectrum of practices and will build their own reputation on the type of work they show, but are unlikely to show work by a new artist that is too similar to someone else on their books. Whilst it is important to keep up with current trends in making and thinking it is far more important to maintain your integrity and stick to your guns. What

curators, commissioners and agencies alike are looking for is innovative quality not 'more of the same'.

Once you have identified a number of galleries or agencies that you think might be interested find out how they prefer to receive proposals and who the best person might be to contact. Visit spaces and build up relationships. A bi-monthly newsletter keeping people up to date with your work is a valuable tool and can be done for free via platforms like Mailchimp. Streamlining the different media options means that you will build up a unique database that is personal to you – Twitter followers often become mailing list subscribers and Facebook friends (for your business page) can link to your website and be directly invited to events. If you aren't sure how best to make use of the different platforms, or how to develop your potential audiences in general there are many arts organisations providing online or actual advice sessions to guide you through. The Crafts Council is a first port of call for most makers but other organisations include a-n – The Artists Information Company who, as well as having a comprehensive website covering everything from how much to charge to online contract toolkits also enable networking events and professional development sessions across the UK. They also provide a variety of affordable insurance options through their membership scheme. DACS protects the rights of artists and helps ensure that any royalties are paid over. Artquest is aimed at London based artists but has an international profile and through its website shares the resources, networks and opportunities you need to develop your practice. Whilst all this may feel like a minefield when you first graduate all of the organisations are geared to artists and makers at different points in their careers and with many, many years experience behind them can quickly point you in the right direction. But you need to be an active participant in your own career development and determine your own path.

*Rising Stars* is an apt title for arts practice in general – we should all be continually striving to be innovative without compromising quality. The makers selected for the exhibition show huge promise and are on their way to achieving this ambition. With continued enthusiasm, dedication and commitment from them and the communities that support contemporary arts practice we uphold, celebrate and advocate for the on-going importance of creative ambition in the United Kingdom.

**Lucy Day**
Day + Gluckman

*Lucy Day is one half of Day + Gluckman, an independent curatorial partnership. Both trained as artists, Day+Gluckman have been working together curating contemporary art projects and exhibitions since 2006. From museum-based exhibitions to collaborations with old master dealers, the duo has worked with over 200 artists in diverse environments. Day is also an advisor to A-N – the artists information company and lectures on curating and artists professional development. She is a Visiting Practitioner at Wimbledon College of Art (UAL).*

*www.dayandgluckman.co.uk*
*www.sinopticon.org*

# Portfolio Careers: A View to Contemporary Crafts over the Past Thirty Years

As Director of the Bluecoat Display Centre in Liverpool I have seen many changes in the Contemporary Craft scene over the past 25 years, but by far the biggest changes, and those I consider most relevant to graduates today have been the emergence of "Portfolio Careers" and, more obviously the increased use of new technologies.

Both areas have led to far better communication and networking links, but have put extra pressure on the makers to effectively manage their time.

When I first arrived in the sector, the majority of makers seemed to be working all hours in studios that were often in idyllic rural situations. It appeared for some to be a peaceful, isolated and often frugal existence. Occasionally, too, there were studio assistants on apprenticeship-type schemes. In those pre-internet days sans websites, digital photography and e-mail attachments, I would often drive around the country viewing work in the studio environment and as a gallerist select pieces for the Bluecoat Display Centre, both for our exhibitions and our shop.

Now the digital revolution has well and truly arrived, makers are able to work in various locations and even different countries and still display their work to us quickly and effectively. The younger generation of makers obviously seek out and thrive on the new digital interfaces, but even the more-established in contemporary craft find that the technology allows them greater freedom, with a number of UK artists moving to rural areas of Europe to raise their families, but still managing to effectively run their businesses, particularly if producing

small, easily transportable pieces such as jewellery or carved wood.

These days, new graduates tend to come out of university with more sophisticated skills, and a greater awareness of the reality of working life, perhaps as a result of the recession and increased education costs.

Alice Kettle, the well-established embroiderer, tells how difficult she found the transition, years ago. "I left college deeply submerged in my work, my head full of dreams. I just wanted to sew; I knew nothing of business or how to earn money. I know a lot more now which I wish I had known then."[1]

It seems that increasingly the idea of a single job for life is an out-of-date concept, and not something that would fit the contemporary lifestyle. There are many advantages to having a portfolio, or mixed- strand career; it can reduce risk by giving a balance of employment and self-employment. After a time of struggle, making large ambitious hangings, Alice Kettle has a career today that involves many different strands of work including lecturing, teaching, writing, designing, collaborating with others, consultating and curating. The large embroideries that she originally produced were difficult to sell, but gained her prestigious exhibitions that in turn led to people taking notice, and opportunities coming her way. Many of the changes of direction were a result of her personal lifestyle; having children, being a single mother, needing affordable workshop space, hitting deadlines, even dealing with repetitive strain injury. She had to rethink her working practices and to learn new skills with the development of new technologies.

A career as full as Alice Kettle's illustrates how important discipline and organisation are when running a portfolio career. This view is endorsed by time management expert Peter Turla's analogy that managing multiple projects is like being the parent of a large family that you have to feed, "Each aspect of your job can be like another child that needs nurturing. You can't neglect any one of the 'children' and expect to have a healthy family."[2]

To survive and thrive in these days of fast changing circumstances and global economies requires entrepreneurial skill, flexibility and the need to embrace change.

Young graduates with a craft related degree, who make up of 60% of UK makers, are now finishing their studies with sizable debts. In reality they need a regular income to survive (as 87% will be working as sole traders,[3]) and these businesses inevitably take a period of time to become established and hopefully successful. Another income strand may take pressure off while this evolves. Graduates must analyse their specific financial needs and artistic values and to find compatible lifework for themselves.

A typical example of this can be seen in the London based ceramicist Grant Aston, who on leaving the RCA had been a student for eight years and tells how, "I wanted a new creative challenge but also needed to earn money, though it was always the plan to get back to being an artist". Grant was keen to learn new skills and gained employment as a specialist decorator for various companies who valued his aesthetic eye. He now has a new portfolio of skills to offer which include furniture restoration, paint finishes, polished-plastering and gilding. He has experience of running large projects in both the UK and abroad. Grant more recently ran a workshop for a company that produces decorative mirrors and restores antiques, and says," I enjoy my job and have a lot of independence at the workshop. I place a lot of value in the skills I have - many of them are transferable across to my art practice".[4]

Another emerging artist, Drew Markou, who makes art jewellery and functional and non-functional objects, tells how he never set out to have a portfolio career, it just naturally evolved. Transferable skills made this a feasible proposition. He, too, works as a restorer, but this time for a specialist vintage car headlamp company and finds this gives him a constant, steady and reliable monthly income; while also challenging his metal working skills, "...as well as allowing me to become more familiar with other industry professionals such as spinners, casters, engravers, glass cutters and may more depending on the restoration job"[5].

Drew also works as a visiting lecturer at various universities and has a great passion for teaching, "I will always want to continue this, as not only do I greatly enjoy it, but it keeps my head in an academic zone and helps me to constantly evaluate my own practice and push my thinking forward"[6]. He feels it is important to see the subject field objectively and to explore how it is grows and develops. On top of all this he also manages to do garden designs and horticultural consultancy.

More opportunities for building a portfolio career will arise as more companies source freelance working. This can be a flexible solution: it does not affect their overheads, and enables them to employ individuals for set projects on contract.

A relatively recent development, partly brought about by the recession and the growth in unemployment during the last five years, has been the re-evaluation of the apprenticeship scheme. Cockpit Arts Studio's are currently developing a scheme that will involve apprentices working with different artists in their group studio, helping young makers gain new skills and experience.

Also worth considering is having a career that will give you another perspective on the Contemporary Crafts infrastructure. The majority of sales still occur in retail spaces, typically in a gallery, an exhibition space, or a specialist shop. It is well worth exploring local opportunities for part-time work. Many employers are pleased to accommodate individuals who have a craft related degree or practice. Makers can give informed opinion to potential customers and collectors. Traditionally, these businesses have just a small team. Holiday and sickness cover is often an important requirement. An internship or voluntary position is also worth considering initially. If opportunities for paid work arise, you may already have the necessary skills and experience and be in a strong position to fill a vacant post.

Makers thus employed will acquire invaluable information about the market and buying habits of collectors and enthusiasts. This can then feed into their business. It can

teach just what information needs to be sent to a gallery to maximise chances of having work accepted. Often simple communication procedures lead to a productive working relationship between maker and gallerist.

Makers working part time in gallery/retail sectors have said it helps to create a balance between contact and isolation. With the vast majority of makers being sole traders, long spells of working alone can lead to them feeling cut-off from other people, and a day or two a week in a more sociable field can assist with counter balancing this.

Many younger makers also take advantage of the opportunity to be based in urban group studios, often with support for business development, and a good social life is part of the package. After the close-knit support of university life this can be a good way to develop your career, and with the increased networking, inevitably more opportunities can come your way.

Another example of how new technologies can be useful is illustrated by ceramicist Sara Flynn who, when working in rural Ireland, needed and appreciated the silence that came with it, but felt socially isolated and so resorted to a Skype call every morning over coffee with artist friends. It made the difference to their working days.

Drew Markou has used technology to assist with his marketing and business. In Project 100, using one set of materials he produced one hundred individual items of sculptural art jewellery (which he sold for £10 each). Filmed on a web-cam, people watched him as he worked through the 24 hours to achieve his target, often purchasing pieces as they were being produced. He acquired many more potential collectors and an increased mailing list for future projects.

However, it is not plain sailing. If you are to consider working in the contemporary craft sector do be aware that the average net profit for a maker in England is less than £9,000 per year after overheads . A portfolio career may be essential. For any maker who considers such this career an efficient system of managing the various strands of work is essential, including marketing and self-marketing. The maker has to allow greater administration time for all of this.

Reflecting on the difficulties of having a portfolio career, Alice Kettle finds, ironically, "Sometimes the hardest part now is to keep enough time to stitch, which is all I ever wanted to do". Grant Aston echoes these frustrations telling how, "My goal and biggest challenge is to be able to free up more time to spend in my studio.

This seems to be a universal challenge for any emerging artist who is financially independent".

Drew Markou, however, points to the positives, "I find having a portfolio career exceptionally important as it keeps my research and inspiration pools fresh and ever increasing. Social media sites such as Facebook and Twitter show how beneficial networking can be, but I find that by having a portfolio career I'm able to do a lot of this networking naturally in real life due to all the people that I interact with in the different areas I'm in".

For all *Rising Stars* I would recommend you follow your star. While the financial rewards might not be huge at the beginning, the level of personal fulfilment increases throughout your life. As Grayson Perry said in the Reith Lectures," If somebody offers you some little exhibition or little part in a group show or a little opportunity, you take it, you take it, you take it because you never know..."

**Dr Maureen Bampton**
Director, Bluecoat Display Centre, Liverpool

References:
1. Personal correspondence, Alice Kettle – Maureen Bampton, 06.11.13
2. On line quotation.
3. Craft in an Age of Change: Summary Report, Crafts Council BOP consulting, February 2012.
4. Personal correspondence, Grant Aston – Maureen Bampton, 28.10.13.
5. Personal correspondence, Drew Markou – Maureen Bampton,31.10.13.
6. Ditto.

# Stepping to success:
## Notes for Emerging and Developing Makers

Rebecca Skeels is a jeweller based in Farnham, Surrey. She is a meticulous designer-maker with a strong desire for knowledge of new materials and processes, and believes in openly sharing her enthusiasm and experience through varied teaching methods. Her post as Subject Leader for Post Graduate Courses in the School of Craft and Design at the University for the Creative Arts in Farnham enables Rebecca to work at undergraduate and postgraduate levels. She teaches students on continually developing courses, by sharing knowledge with craft practitioners and artists of the future.

In addition to her role at the University for the Creative Arts, Rebecca contributes to art and craft professions throughout the UK. She is a member of the Board of Directors for the Association for Contemporary Jewellery (ACJ), enabling her to network and converse with some of the UK's leading jewellers and theorists. She is also a member of the Board of Trustees for the New Ashgate Gallery in Farnham. Rebecca helps in assisting the running of events such as the Rising Stars touring exhibition that runs alongside a symposium, mentoring and commission opportunities. More recently, Rebecca was elected to the executive committee for the Hand Engravers Association, an organisation committed to raising the awareness of the historic trade and encouraging new makers to learn traditional hand engraving skills. Rebecca also teaches short courses, ad hoc classes and one to one classes at 318 Ceramics in Wrecclesham, Surrey, making jewellery and metalsmithing accessible to people of all ages, abilities and backgrounds.

Over the past 20 years, Rebecca has been the sole proprietor of SKEELS, a developing jewellery and product design company. This has allowed Rebecca to work on commissions as well as her collections ranging from handmade cufflinks, pendants and furniture to installations in public spaces. Her work is exhibited through galleries, shops, craft shows and trade exhibitions in the UK and abroad.  Rebecca's research and experimentation with alternative materials inspired her to produce a number of one-off pieces of jewellery to complement her existing ranges. This led to organising and running a symposium/exchange with the Jewellers and Silversmiths Network (JSN) and the Critique Collective Network in San Francisco in 2010. The JSN is a group run by its members for its members with the aim of sharing experience and knowledge. Rebecca intends to expand her recent collections with more research and experimentation, taking the opportunity to use new, developing and different materials and technologies. Research will be undertaken to develop new methods in which jewellery and metalwork are taught.

Rebecca's advice below is from her experiences, reading, writing, knowledge and observations. She hopes that each person reading this article will take something away that will help them now and in the future to develop their own careers; whether they are starting from scratch or developing their businesses in new directions. Success should be measured in terms of developing a career that enables you to do what you love and enjoy.

Small creative businesses are as much about balance of duties as they are about making something desirable and well crafted. New tools are continuously becoming available to help run, publicise and manage a business smoothly and efficiently. This is similar to many of the craft trades, unlike some trades the new processes are added to our toolbox and skills rather than replacing them, making more choices available. At first this can seem overwhelming, but with planning, judgment and careful selection this will all help achieve your main aims. Assess what tools your business requires in order to get you where you want to be.

Each person is unique, making every business plan and structure unique; this is why each individual needs to find a personal way of working and developing to help their business grow. It is worth spending time and effort at various points in our careers to decide which direction to go in and how to achieve our aims. Business people as well as their businesses need to constantly to grow and develop, sometimes in small gradual steps and on other occasions in bold, courageous challenging leaps. Growing a business does not always mean making it bigger or becoming famous, it can mean changing to enable it to continue to do what is needed or desired. Our environment is evolving, people's tastes and ideals, the economic climate, the market or even how we feel about it personally will change. Businesses need to be able to grow along with these changes to survive; something that was successful in the past may not be the answer to great success in the future.

Keeping on track and not getting distracted is important. Ending up on a different path than intended can easily happen, it may be a better path or it may mean disaster.

Therefore, it is advisable to write a business plan. Business plans are useful for funding opportunities, opening bank accounts or getting premises, but they are most useful for the author and for running the business. A business plan can begin by writing everything down on paper to enable an idea to form a structure and focus. Always remember that the plan is not set in stone and may need to be flexible to allow for changes and alterations as learning and development takes place. Business plans can be rewritten as situations change, but do not put off writing the plan just because it will change; it is never a waste of time. Consider what you really want to do, what you enjoy and how you can have fun.

Short-term plans need be more comprehensive; include details to achieve the main aim. Use a time planner to construct a timetable for the year, including deadlines for different aspects of the business, for example market research, making, trade shows, exhibitions and designing. It is important to keep to this plan; allow yourself time to run the business and focus on different aspects. Line up jobs and commissions rather than take on too much at one time or thinking of each job in isolation.

Restrict your internet and phone time to defined time slots. Online activities can take up more time than you realise, a quick check to see if someone has responded to an online post also includes efforts to go to the post and then time to get the mind back to your original focus. Getting your mind back on track after a distraction can take more than double the time away.

Plan to allow time for yourself, make sure breaks are taken as well as designing, research and drawing activities are included. These aspects help reflection, development and thinking which will save time in the long term. A business cannot survive if an individual has to work all hours, does not get enough sleep and never allows time to develop, it is not sustainable over a longer term. Health and fitness is important, be prepared and in good health for the next and subsequent jobs.

Time to network is valuable; this can include visiting exhibitions, symposiums, lectures, and talking to other makers. Do not restrict network time to online activities only; more personal development, enjoyment and unexpected learning takes place face to face. Networking can help promote individuals and small businesses and lead to unexpected opportunities. If you find it hard to network, try to think of it in different terms. When in conversation with anyone consider what may be achieved from the encounter, for example; meeting local makers, which suppliers do they recommend, or do they endorse a good exhibition, could a stand be shared at a new show together?

Costing items to sell is challenging but something well worth putting in time to give you confidence in your margins. Networking may help, but other practitioners are likely to be reluctant in giving advice, they may not be confident themselves, not want others to judge them or maybe hesitant to give advice as your pieces fit in a different context to theirs. Pricing an item will get quicker and easier the more experience you have.

The first step is to understand how much money is required to survive. List all the items on one page you spend money on throughout the year, for example rent, food, going out and bills. Do not include anything that is related to your business, then add all of the costs up and put the total at the bottom of the page. On the second page, list all costs to keep your business open, include workshop rent and bills, marketing, photography, and travel, do not include commissions or projects. Again, put the total at the bottom of the page.

On the third page work out how many hours you intend to work over the year, start with the number of weeks and remember to allocate time for holidays and potential sickness. How many days will be for work each week, will you work weekends? Then how many hours per day will you work, do not forget to subtract a lunch break. This calculation is helpful: hours worked per day, multiplied by, days worked per week, multiplied by, weeks worked per year, the result is hours worked over the year. At the bottom of this page add the totals from page one and two together, then divide it by the hours worked per year. This result is how much you need to charge per hour if you were working solidly for every hour you wish to work.

Use a fourth page to work out the materials that have or are going to use for an individual job or commission, remember to include everything, special packaging, tests and experiments, moulds, hired equipment, breakages or mistakes, or was anything outsourced. If stock materials are used, how much does it cost to replace them? Include the delivery charge for materials. If there are minimum orders for materials from your suppliers and there is no intention to use the rest, charge for all of it. Next record or estimate the time you will require for each individual job, commission or piece of work. This needs to include every bit of time, imagine an employee of a company and what they do in a working day. Include clearing up for the next job, setting up, designing, calling the customer and meeting with them, getting the commission, travelling to get supplies and researching. Multiply the hours estimated or recorded by the total from the third page and add it to the cost of the materials. This total is the lowest that can be charged for an item.

The final steps are the most challenging. The total so far is the lowest wholesale price you can charge for an item. A wholesale price is what you charge to a retailer, a shop or a gallery. If you are selling to the public you will need to calculate a retail price, this can be achieved by adding anything from 35% to 120%. Research the market and retail customers to see what calculation to apply to your wholesale price. A good practitioner understands the context of their work, where will it end up and who the customers are. This will help when researching what others are charging for similar items, what the customers are willing to pay and where you should be showing and selling your work. Compare your retail price calculation with other similar practitioners' prices, if the result is much higher, you need to cut costs somewhere. The main aim is to be in a position to add a profit, as practitioners need at least a small margin of profit to grow and develop. Profit will allow for the development of new ideas and work, purchase of new equipment, taking work in new directions and to continue on the journey towards your main aim for your business and you as a practitioner.

This advice is only touching on a few elements of running a business, there are many books, networks, classes and mentoring programmes and help available. Read the books that you find useful, network, learn and develop in the way that works for you and most of all good luck with your new venture and the growing of your business.

**Rebecca Skeels**
Subject Leader for Post Graduate School of Craft and Design, University for the Creative Arts, Farnham

# Élodie Alexandre

**2013 MA Ceramics,** Cardiff Metropolitan University.
**2011 BA Ceramics,** Cardiff Metropolitan University.

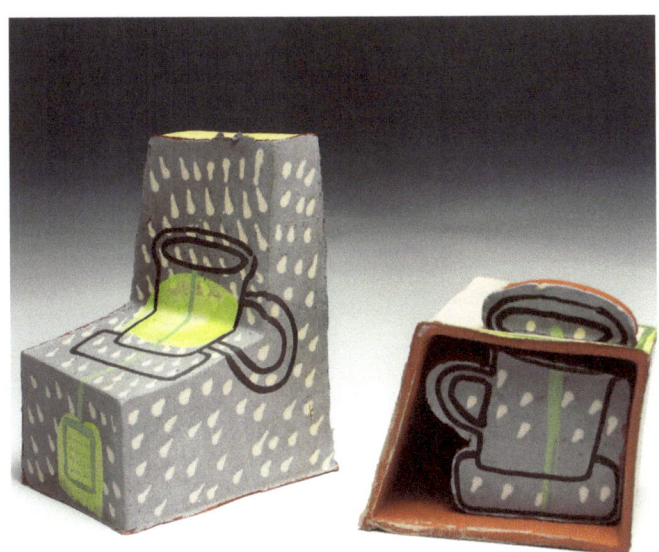

*The tea that tasted of monsoon*
Terracotta and vitreous slips

Élodie Alexandre's work investigates the relationship between drawing and making in ceramics, at a point of oscillation between the two and three dimensional. This exploration is envisaged as a translation process, comparable to the act of translating one language into another: where what is looked at is the grey area that separates and unifies, the territory of the 'in between' rather than the points of departure and arrival.

The objects that arise from this journey can be seen as valid attempts, like multiple ways of translating. They allow lines to be reinvented and visual conversations to emerge. The images used are based on personal memories of everyday objects and the emotions attached to them. Creating space for discovery and meandering, they evoke something belonging to the subtle and the felt and map a territory that is mysterious yet familiar, personal yet universal.

Élodie Alexandre lives and works in Devon.

# Elizabeth Ashdown

**2013 BA Textile Design (woven),** Central St Martins College of Art and Design.

Elizabeth Ashdown specialises in producing innovative and contemporary hand woven, mixed media Passementerie which blurs the boundaries between art, fashion, architecture and design.

Elizabeth utilises vibrant colour, unusual materials and exquisite hand craftsmanship to produce beautiful and highly tactile Passementerie art pieces that range from 1 inch to 2.5 inches wide, and between 30" and 60" long. For her latest collection, *Stitched Connections*, Elizabeth undertook extensive research into military and Tudor embroidery, combing the colour palette, textures and forms of these artefacts with the fluorescent highlights and brights found on jukebox circuit boards and the gleaming metallics of motorbike engines. The collection utilises a wide range of techniques and practices such as kumihimo, intricate on loom pleating, fringing, corduroy and hand lacing in order to produce a collection that updates and reinterprets historical military influences for a contemporary audience.

Elizabeth's use of materials has largely been informed by the materials used on traditional embroidered military garments such as bullion springs, gold work threads and textile metals. These more traditional materials have been combined with rock climbing paracord, leathers, lurex, polyester, silks and reflective yarns.

Elizabeth Ashdown lives and works in Lingfield, Surrey.

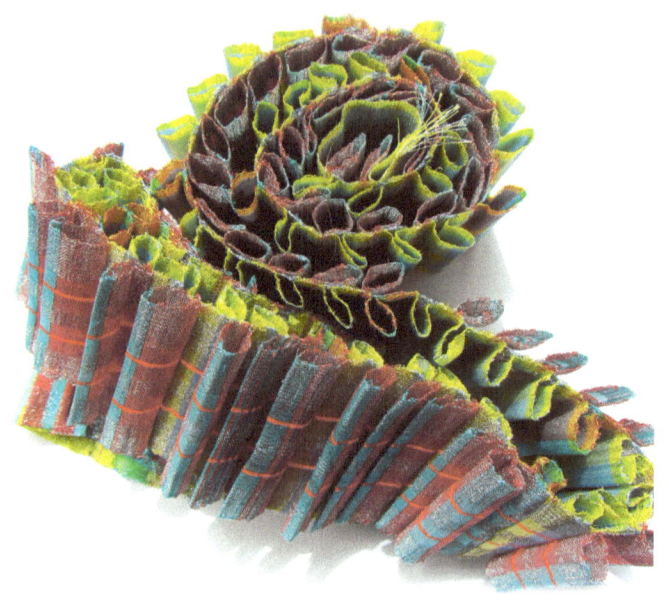

*Trafalgar*
Woven textiles

# Juliette Bigley

**2013 BA Silversmithing,** Cass School of Art, Architecture and Design.

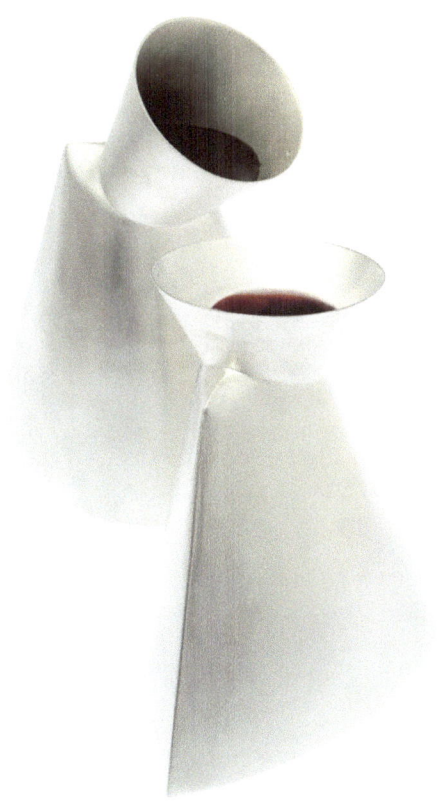

*Water and Wine Carafes*
Silver plate

Our lives are lived through, brightened and coloured by the objects with which we surround ourselves. These objects' characters and our interactions with them fascinate Juliette Bigley.

We use favourite objects, some obvious, some seemingly inconsequential, to augment our experiences, emotions and thoughts. These frequently over-looked everyday companions make our tea more warming, our food taste better and add a depth to our experiences that we may not know is there until an a favourite object-friend is lost or broken and the sense of loss that accompanies this tells of the ability that these objects have to transform not only themselves but our relationship to them.

Juliette's work explores these transformations as well as the relationships and interactions that characterise them and she is particularly interested in what the way in which we see, interpret and interact with forms tells us about ourselves and the rituals – small or large – with which we fill our lives.

Working in both silver and base metals, Juliette's work is both sculptural and functional, and is characterised by a focus on line and form. All of her work is characterised by relationships: within the piece, between the piece and the viewer or between the pieces themselves.

Juliette Bigley lives and work in London.

# Rachel Britch

**2013 BA Embroidery,** Manchester Metropolitan University.

Rachel Britch's practice focuses on current global issues, specifically on sustainability and growing urban populations. Working with these ideas allows her to develop interior hand crafted objects that are concept lead. Through her degree Rachel developed precision making skills and found her passion for large scale installations and site-specific sculpture.

Using re-cycled and biodegradable materials connected without chemicals or adhesives sheds a light on ideas surrounding over consumption and waste. Objects are constructed out of repeated elements, building up to create something complex out of simple units. Through this way of working unlikely or waste materials are used to create innovative, hand crafted objects.

Rachel's practice straddles both conceptual design and handmade craft sectors, creating products that are beautiful and ethical.

Rachel Britch lives and works in Manchester.

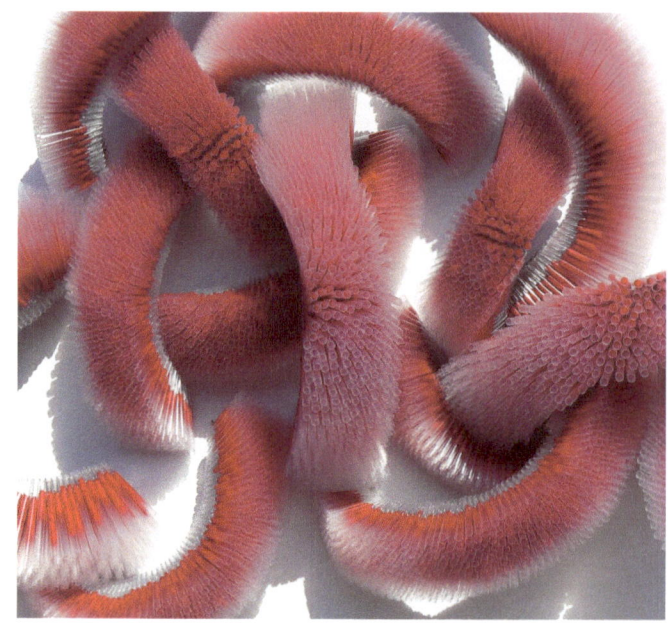

*RED interior wall piece*
This wall mounted piece is made from
100% bio plastic straws, paper clips and wool

# Jessica Coleman

**2013 MA Textile Design,** Royal College of Art.
**2010 BA Fine Art,** Central St Martins.

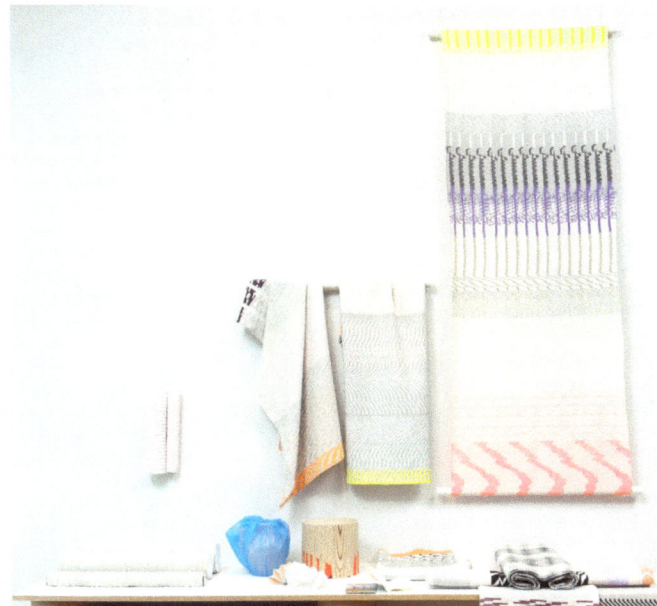

From left, *Diffusion, Diffusion Orange, AV1 Pink, AV1 Blue, AV1 Purple*
Merino wool, ceramic and embroidery thread, silk crepe,
various dimensions

Jessica Coleman's practice is an investigation of visual sensations. Her starting points for ideas are formed by play, be it with materials or research matter. Experimental methods are used to develop colour and surface, particularly within weave and embroidery. Jessica's approach is open-ended and can be applied to multiple disciplines and questions such as interiors, wearable or autonomous artworks.

For the most recent collection entitled *AV1*, Jessica generated designs by feeding pulses of sound into a cathode ray tube television and photographing the results.

From these designs, Jessica produced densely patterned lamb's wool blankets and experimental jacquard fabric samples using merino wool and ceramic coated embroidery thread.

Jessica also produced the embroidery pieces *Diffusion* and *Diffusion Orange*, derived from the pattern and luminous sensation of the *AV1* series photographs. Matt textured neutral thread is layered over bright fluorescents in dense tightly packed undulating lines. The colours blend together to create hazy unfamiliar tones.

Jessica Coleman lives and works in London.

# Anna Collette Hunt

**2009 BA Decorative Arts,** Nottingham Trent University.

Anna Collette Hunt uses clay to create vivid worlds you can step into. They may be universes or they may be mere fragments, it depends on how much she chooses to reveal. Anna tells whimsical stories and invents legends to illustrate the ceramic pieces. The scenes and compositions captured upon the surfaces speak of historic grandeur and past traditions whilst on closer inspection whisper darker sentiments delicately into your ear.

The curiously odd ceramics radiate her preoccupation with historic houses for their excessive decoration, opulence, and obsessive natural history collections and specimens. Anna collects characters from such places; it could be a statue, a piece of furniture or a pattern. Drawings of these elements are playfully translated onto the clay. Scale and setting are often distorted to keep the images fresh and stimulating. Visual depth is achieved through the many layers of colours, markings and transfers that are fired upon the ceramic surface.

Alongside her two dimensional collection of illustrative ceramics Anna creates large scale installations.

Anna Collette Hunt lives and works in Nottingham.

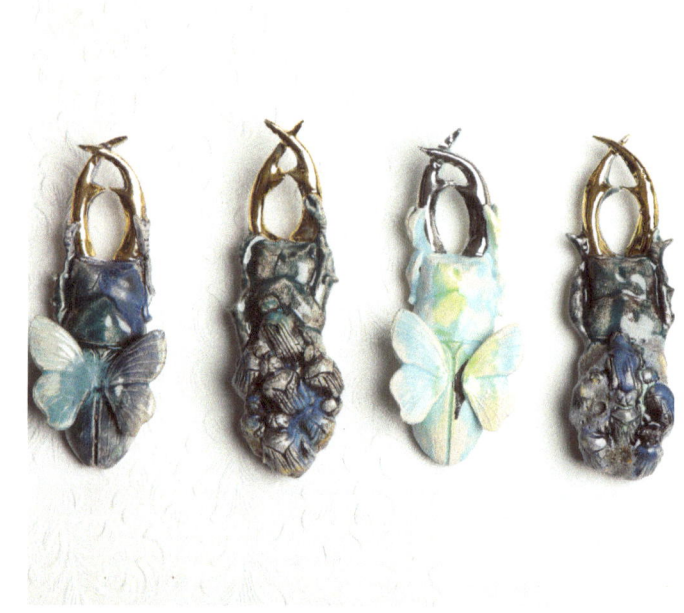

*Magical Stag Beetles*
Ceramic with precious metal lustres

# Polly Collins

**2013 BA Jewellery and Silversmithing,** Edinburgh College of Art.

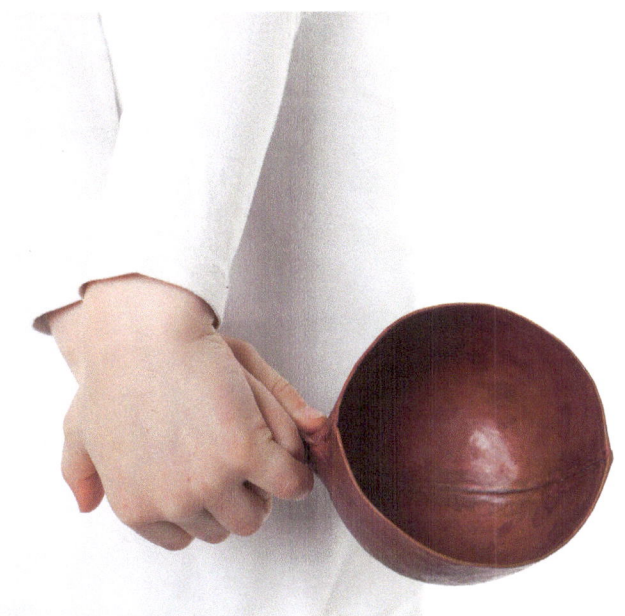

Polly Collins, *'Holding the Greedy Spout'*
Copper
Photographer Konrad Mielniczuk

Polly Collins considers a world in which we are friends with our utensils, where we want to spend time with them and to nurture them; a place where we slow down a bit. These speculative forms invite us to reflect on a different pace of living through their ambiguity in both material and function, sparking a conversation between user and object. The creature-like appearance of the vessels, as well as the different personalities and temperaments they have, are there to encourage this conversation to continue.

Polly works predominantly in sheet metal, yet treats it like textile; creating seams and gussets into soft forms. She rolls print directly from canvas, she alters her hammers so they give a texture of textile and she make chasing tools that give this effect. Polly challenges the conventions of silversmithing through her approach, yet still utilises the traditional palette of techniques.

Polly is interested in challenging the expectations of a material; forming the cold and hard into something comforting and warm.

Polly Collins lives and works in Edinburgh.

# Brittany Delany

**2012 BA Decorative Arts,** Nottingham Trent University.

Brittany Delany creates functional porcelain tableware, decorations and jewellery by slip-casting and slabbuilding. Using porcelain as a medium, she exaggerates its translucent quality and the fragile effects that can be produced.

Originally taking inspiration from taxidermy, her first collection of work is delicately stitched together using a variety of metals. Metals are also used to create colours in the smooth white glaze. Each piece is entirely individual and a leather tag stating its casting number hangs from each vessel. Casting seams and strap marks are exaggerated creating a form of decoration.

More recently Brittany has begun introducing colour into her work. The Seasalt collection is inspired by trips to the seaside and the feeling of salt on your skin. Once again exaggerating casting seams, the simple shapes are glazed with frosty blues and greens. All of Brittany's work is functional and glazed. She finds it important to continually move on with her work and is always developing new products.

Brittany Delany lives and works in Stockport, Cheshire.

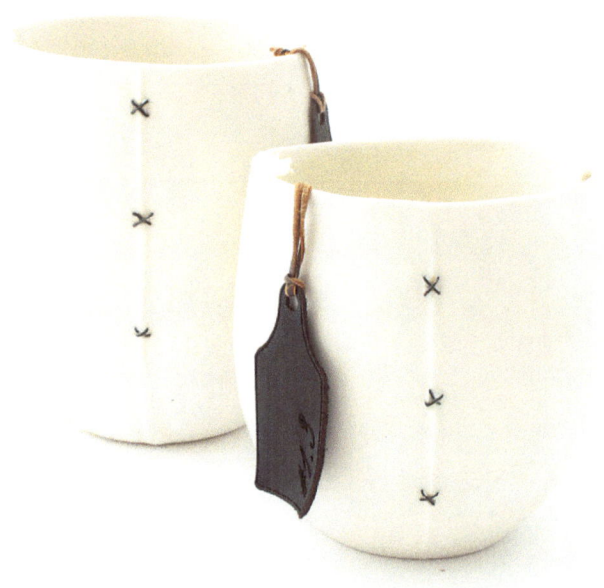

*Small & Medium Taxidermy Vessels*
Porcelain

# Eva Farkasova

**2013 BA Ceramics,** Limerick School of Art and Design.

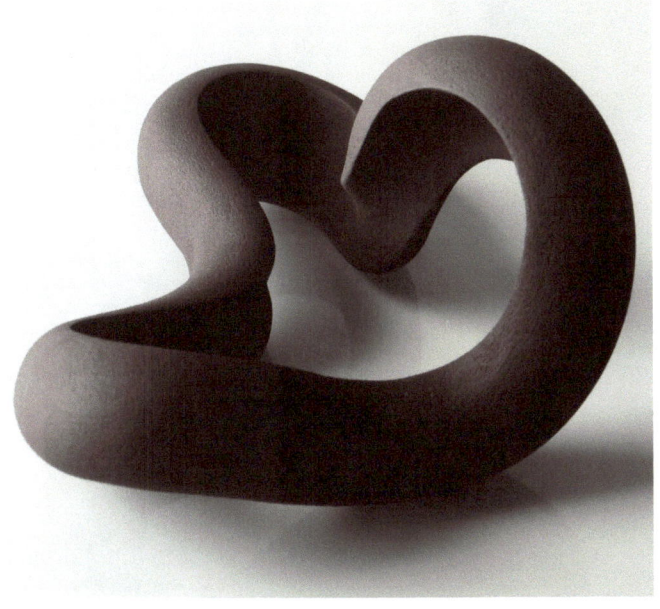

*No. 2, Terracotta*

Nature and the shapes found within it are Eva Farkasova's primary inspiration. Through her work Eva aims to remind the viewer of the feelings experienced when out in nature: sense of fresh air, peace and freedom. These feelings are calming, comforting and relaxing.

We live in a busy highly technological world where nature is often forgotten. Eva's ceramic forms are intended to evoke and restore natural environment. Recreating objects that have visual harmony and tactile seduction, qualities that impact positively on our psychological and emotional well-being is the aim of these pieces.

Eva Farkasova lives and works in Limerick, Ireland.

# Jessica Frost

**2013 BA Contemporary Jewellery,** University for the Creative Arts, Rochester.

The running theme throughout Jessica Frost's work is structure, the form of buildings and their surroundings. Jessica photographs urban scenarios, looking for forms that can be seen in the midst of different environments.

Jessica explores different forms, colours, and materials that can be linked to the images, silicone, wood and metal. The pieces are composed of simple and complex shapes and a variety of scales. She has an interest in the juxtapositions that are created through material, colour, shape and form, for example hollow next to solid and wood next to silicone.

For that reason Jessica has been looking at the work of Jantje Fleischhut who uses plastics and metal for the forms and structures of necklaces and brooches. The way Nicolas Cheng layers organic materials 'imperfectly' has also been an inspiration. Another example is Katja Prins, her use of monochrome adds to the simplicity of her shapes and forms, creating these animated and comic like, wearable pieces.

Jessica Frost lives and works in Essex.

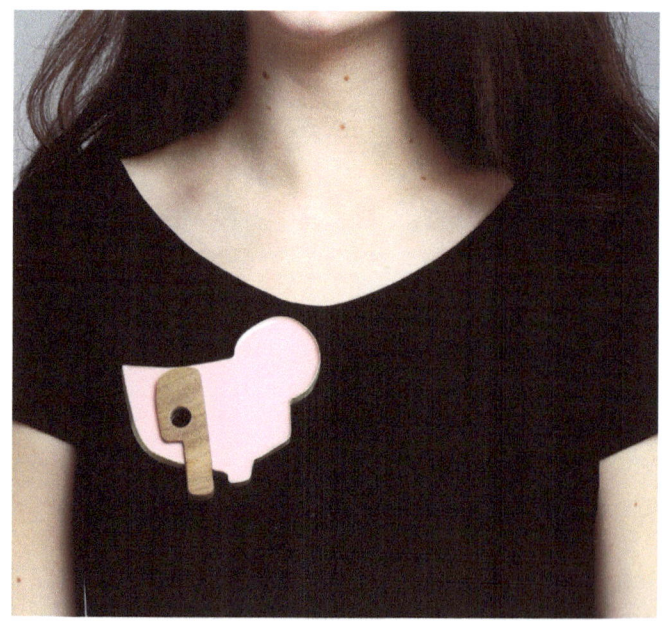

*Pink brooch*
Silicone, metal and walnut wood
Photographer Maria Leao

# Joanna Fronczak

**2012 BA Design for Industry,** Birmingham School of Jewellery.

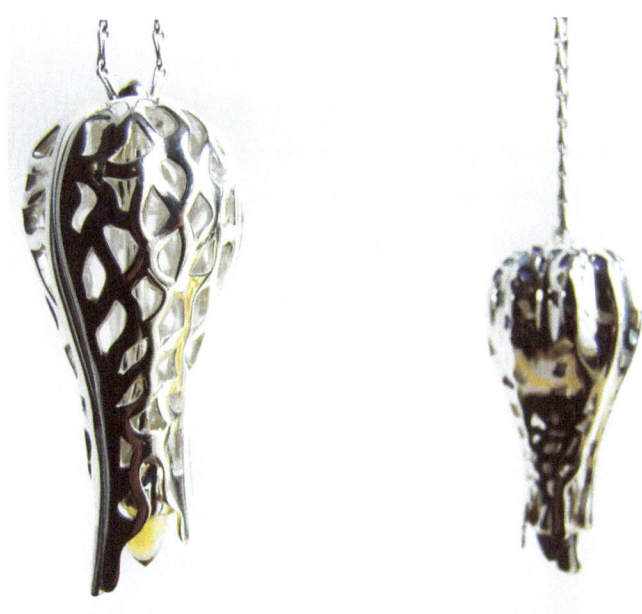

*Ajoure*, interchangeable pendants
Silver, semi-precious stones and enamel (contains 2 pendants in one)

Joanna Fronczak is a jewellery designer and maker from Poland, currently based in the UK, precisely in Birmingham's Jewellery Quarter. Joanna's passion for travel and the experience gained from living in two countries is reflected in her diverse designs. Nature, colour and the behaviour of human beings has a huge impact on Joanna's pieces.

Joanna has recently launched a new collection called *Ajouré*, informed by the organic structure of the Chinese lantern plant alongside the fascinating patterns and shapes observed in flowing water. The delicate, dry structures represent the fragility and imperfections of the human race while the water mirrors how people can change. The main focus of the collection is an interchangeable pendant. This two-in-one piece can be worn together or separately.

Joanna's *Weather Brooch* is designed to bring a smile to the face of the wearer by giving a possibility to change the state of the weather. Since the jewellery is more than decoration, the interactive elements create a link between the piece and the wearer who has opportunity to recreate them as desired.

Joanna's love for colour means that her designs very often contain precious and semi-precious stones as well as enamel and anodised aluminium.

Joanna Fronczak lives and works in Birmingham.

# Kerstin Haigh

**2012 BA Silversmithing and Jewellery Design,** London Metropolitan University.

Kerstin Haigh creates sculptural objects and precious jewellery to communicate individual stories or capture the sense of a striking moment. Things litter our homes. Heirlooms, experiences and ephemera collected through life are symbols, evoking moments in time and our memories. Natural elements mark and transform the environment with growth and decay. These layers look different in the urban landscape, the old stories are contained beneath modernity, archived in books and photographs, each are ghosts; physical structures that once occupied a space.

By designing sculptural items, containers and jewellery, Kerstin communicate stories and special significance. Patterns, images, textures and materials provide identified references which serve to punctuate the visual language. Experimentation with modern and ancient techniques like lazer etching, 3D printing, lost wax casting and forging, inform the progress. Kerstin pushes her specialism of kiln fired enamel and its conventional applications. Some pieces are composed using precious materials and others by applying combined mixed media. The delightful palette of nature and intriguing reflections of life that surround us inspires her small collections.

Kerstin Haigh lives and works in London.

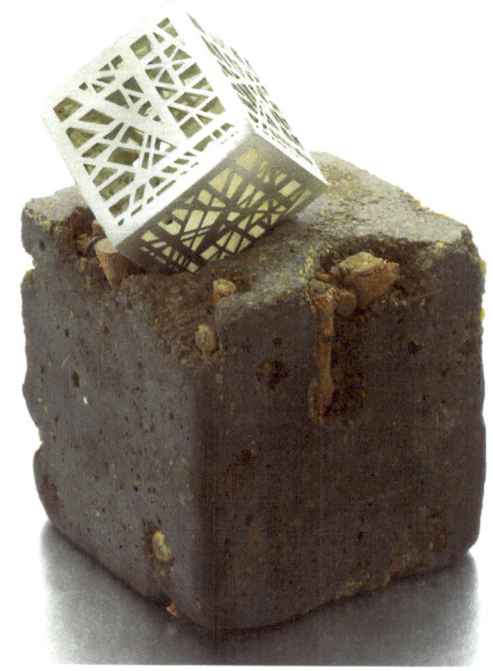

*Burma Scaffold on cement block*

# Ruth Harrison

**2013 BA Ceramics,** Plymouth School of Art.

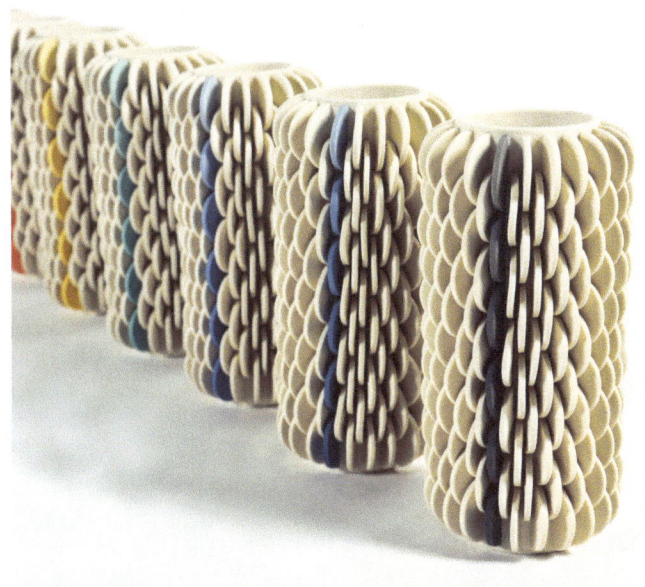

*Colour Strip* collection
Porcelain and coloured body stain

Ruth Harrison uses porcelain to create sculptural forms using repeated elements. She is interested in symmetry and the idea of taking one shape and multiplying it many times over or around a cylinder. She chooses to use porcelain due to its white body when fired to 1260°c. Porcelain also works very well with coloured stain which she uses for some of her collections.

Ruth draws the attention of the viewer to a section or strip of the finished piece using colour, texture or pattern which is added to the piece as it is being made. Each disk is hand cut using a cookie cutter from 3mm thick slabs of porcelain which are then cut in half, sponged, scored, slipped and attached to a slip-cast cylinder. Her work evokes the childhood memory of running a hand or stick along a fence.

Ruth Harrison lives and work in Plymouth, Devon.

# Mirka Janeckova

**2013 BA Silversmithing and Jewellery,** Glasgow School of Art.

Mirka Janeckova is a Czech jeweller who sees jewellery as a container for the wearer's emotions, memories and hopes. Mirka's pieces refer to the body in an abstract way, exploring the relationship between people and the subconscious mind.

For her most recent work, Mirka was inspired by the colour white, surrealism and deep sea. White materials such as porcelain, silver, aluminium and textiles create playful, poetic pieces. White light contains all the others colour of the spectrum - for Mirka it is a symbol of unity. Mirka also experiments with hybrid metal-porcelain jewellery to develop an innovative way of applying traditional metalsmith techniques onto porcelain, for example casting porcelain in place and cloisonné enamel on porcelain.

Mirka Janeckova lives and works in Glasgow.

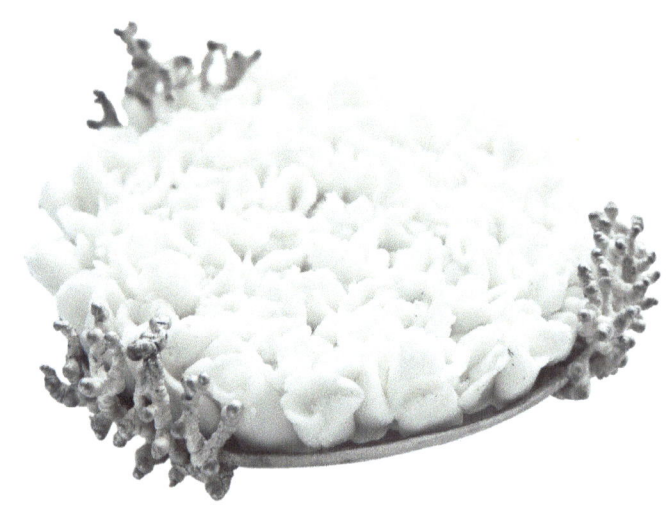

*Brooch*
Porcelain, casted silver

# Anum Khan

**2014 BA Three Dimensional Design (glass),** University for the Creative Arts, Farnham.

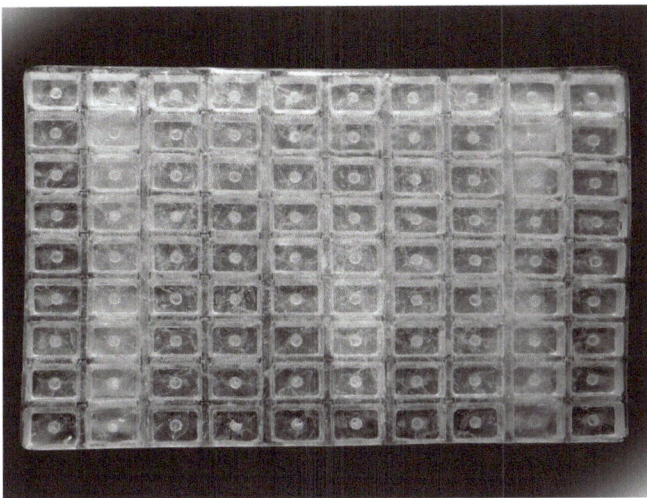

*Ice Table*
Glass, kiln cast

Living in the hustle and bustle of London is stressful and hectic after a busy day, everyone including Anum, hasten to return back home and relax. Anum Khan aims to produce a piece that captures and communicates a sense of stillness, of calm and quiet in a demanding and chaotic world. Anum has chosen water and ice trays as one way to explore the transparency of both water and glass. Water is restful and calming, when frozen as snow and ice it is still and quiet. Glass with heat in the kiln can transform from solid to liquid and back again, as water does with cold in a freezer.

Anum uses the lost wax process for these pieces: casting multiple ice cube trays in wax then using these for a mould that, once the wax is removed, filled with glass in the kiln. The work is then cold worked and bonded with epoxy to create a base.

The top of *Ice Table* is cloudy with veils and hints at movement in the water while the curved, kiln slumped legs create another sense of movement and change as ice becomes water. It can also be placed as a sculptural piece that can enhance an environment as well as being functional.

Anum Khan lives and works in London and Farnham.

# Lisa Larcombe

**2013 BA Three Dimensional Design (metalwork and jewellery),** University for the Creative Arts, Farnham.

Lisa Larcombe's work is a fusion of inspiration, knowledge and skills acquired from her profession as a biomedical scientist and her passion for creative expression through making.

Lisa takes inspiration from anatomical drawings, both human and plant and develops designs by adapting and incorporating the many techniques and skills that she has learnt into the art of designing and making. This gives the work a unique and personal identity. Some of Lisa's work has evolved from a conceptual start point in which she explores bio ethical issues, whilst other pieces explore the wonder of the inner workings of the body.

Lisa's work is often small scale silver and metal jewellery, which she naturally tend towards as a result of her professional practice. The small scale and intimate relationship that jewellery has with the body, makes it an entirely appropriate media for the expression of Lisa's ideas.

Lisa Larcombe lives and works in Surrey.

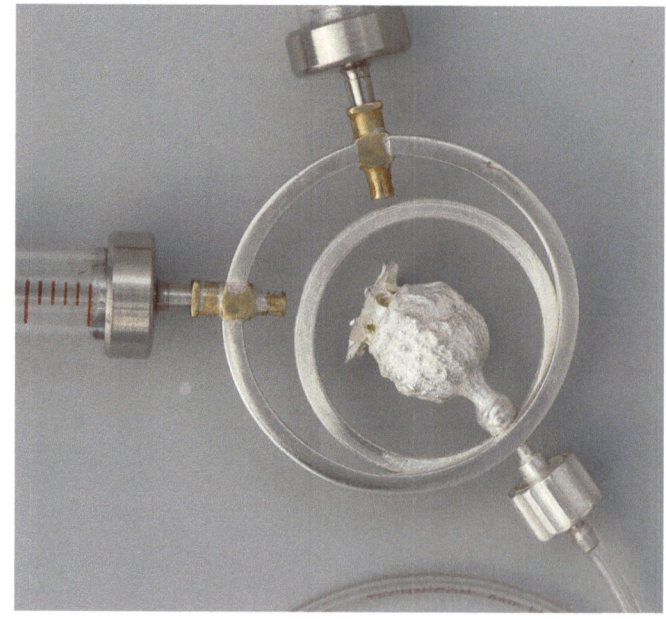

*Science Abuse*
Sterling silver and bronze pendant with latex tubing and medical
syringes on hand cut and fabricated titanium chain maille

# Beatrice Larkin

**2013 BA Textiles (woven),** Royal College of Art, London.

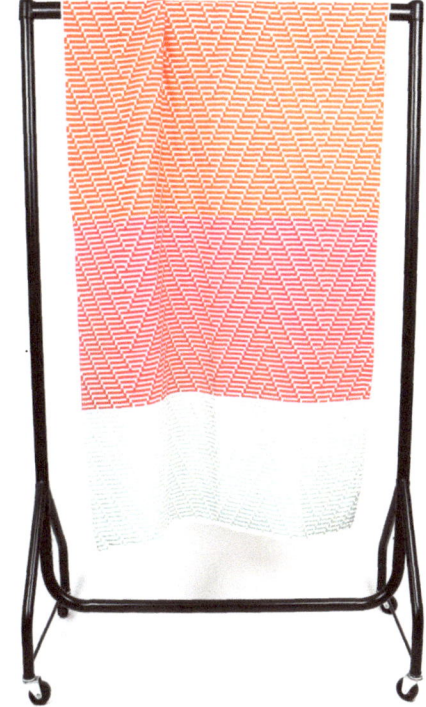

*Bright Herringbone Jacquard*
*Silk and cashwool*

Broken mismatched geometrics and grids have inspired Beatrice Larkin's most recent collection of Jacquard and Dobby woven textile blankets and throws. Some are hand-woven and some woven and finished at mills in the UK.

Predominantly working with a bold monochrome palette, Beatrice has manipulated hand drawings and traditional weave structures, offsetting patterns and scales to meet unexpectedly with the intent to create statement geometrics in a freehand style. Made from wool, cashmere and silk, the finished throws have a desirable handle that conveys quality, honesty and longevity.

Beatrice lives and works in London.

# Anne Laycock

**2011 BA Three Dimensional Design,** Manchester School of Art.

Anne Laycock is a Londoner with a design background and a wealth of multicultural experiences. Anne worked as a successful art director in a leading London advertising agency. Marriage and the birth of two children instigated a change of direction. As a freelancer several creative projects filled the gaps around travelling with and supporting her husband's worldwide career. Anne's home for the majority of the last twenty years has been transient and out of the UK spending time spent in Africa and living in various European countries. These multicultural experiences have inspired and informed her greatly. Now relocated back in the UK in Sheffield the memories of architectural forms, colours and styles express themselves in her range of work today.

Anne is not afraid to break the rules she challenges the materials she works with discovering their inherent qualities and playfully putting them to use. The results are bold, unique, spontaneous, rhythmic and visual graphic, representing a strong personal identity. Her ceramic Scribbles Vessels of extruded lengths of clay coaxed to meander in and out of space are voluminous confusions that trap the eye to explore their captivating and expressive movement. Her *Ceramic Wear* transforms an ordinary black dress to extraordinary.

Anne Laycock lives and works in Sheffield.

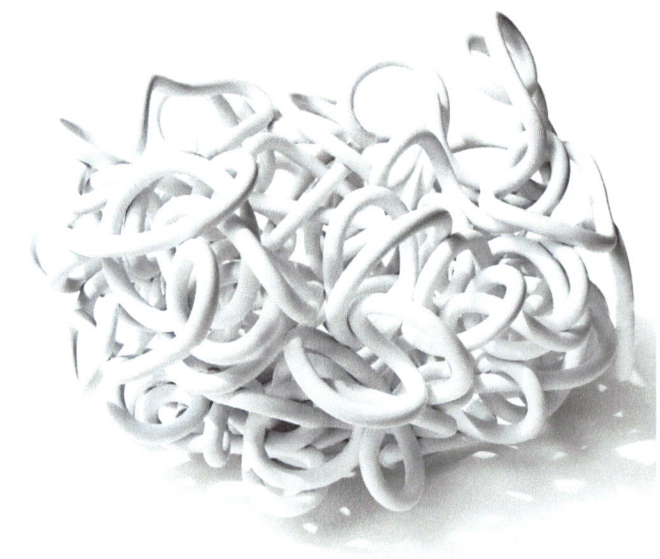

*Scribble Vessel*
Stoneware, ink lacquer

# Beth Lewis-Williams

**2013 MA Design,** Central St Martins.
**2007 BA Ceramics,** Camberwell College of the Arts.

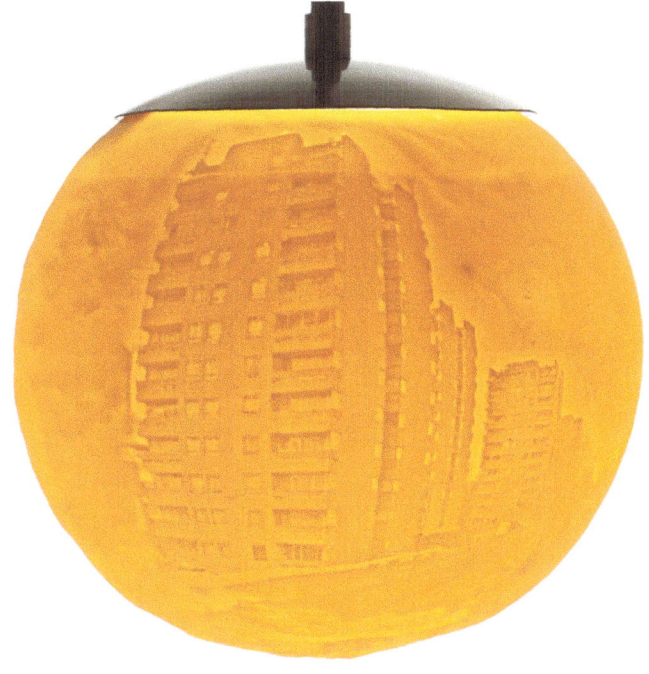

*Tower Block 1*
Hand carved porcelain

Beth Lewis-Williams is showing a collection of porcelain lighting, which exploits the traditional and mysterious technique of lithophanes. The lights are realised using 3D printing technologies and hand carving, the latest LED and lighting controls. They explore urban scenes contrasting current social, environmental, and aesthetic scenes with those of the romantic landscapes featured on 19th century industrially produced domestic ceramics.

Lithophanes were a 19th century passion and were used with an internal light source diffusing through the porcelain creating a gentle play of shadows exposing beautiful, delicate and sculptural images. The widespread emergence of printed landscape patterns on industrial ceramics was driven by the fashion for Chinese and Japanese porcelain, decorated with idyllic and picturesque landscapes. It was in effect a rural nostalgia, the result of a confluence of technological development and urbanisation. Beth's work, in turn, examines our intense urban landscapes though the elegiac atmosphere lithophanes create.

Future work will be structured through a bespoke design and manufacturing service delivering unique lighting features for individual clients.

Beth Lewis-Williams lives and works in London.

# Agnieska Maksymiuk

**2013 HND Jewellery & Silversmithing**, School of Jewellery, Birmingham.
**2010 MA Design for Industry,** Academy of Fine Arts in Gdansk, Poland.

Agnieska Maksymiuk's collection is about the relationship between city and nature. The impact of two different worlds. For example, in the *Windsor Castle Ring* Agnieska is inspired by a colourful garden – the nature surrounding architectural elements of the castle. In the piece *City Ring* the colours work differently. The drawing of the buildings is set in colour and pebbles, which are underneath the street and kept in grey gradation.

Agnieska is also inspired by the British landscape. Agnieska comes from Poland and living in England has been a new experience. She looks at the surroundings like a traveller who discovers a busy city with a lovely river for the first time. Agnieska expresses these feelings in her *London Ring*. Inside the ring you can see a reflection of yourself; this is as if you were inside the city, surrounded by London's greatest monuments. Main landmarks are easy recognisable to the viewer.

Agnieska lives and works in Birmingham.

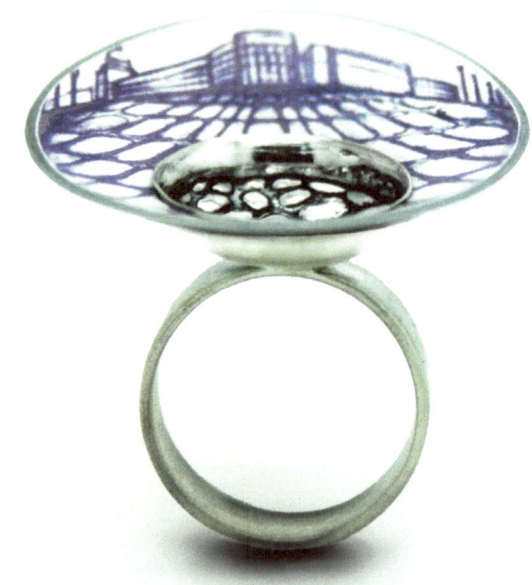

*City Ring*
Silver, aluminium

37

# Elise Menghini

**2013 BA Ceramics**, Bath Spa University.

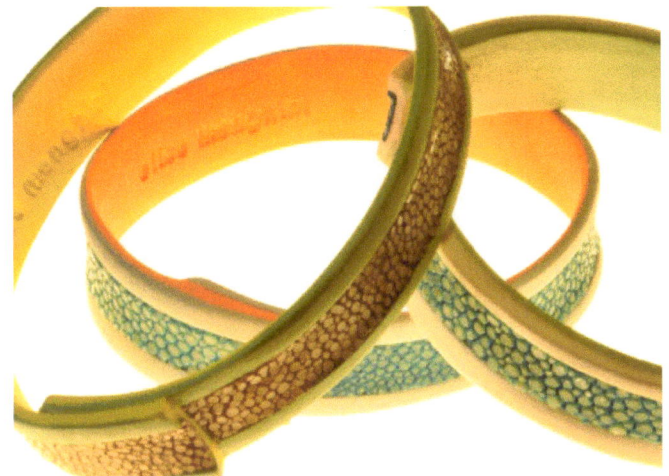

*Porcelain Bangles*
Ceramic and shagreen

Elise Menghini makes playful and intriguing ceramic objects that capture an idea and a sense of place. Everyday, familiar but ignored elements inspire my colourful pieces, while the nature of multiples, produced through her preferred technique of mouldmaking, provide visual order and opportunities for decorative freedom.

Ceramics is Elise's primary material, but her fascination with materials and process has led to the use of different, but complementary media. Wood, metal, paper, acrylic and fish skin are among the varied forms that comprise her work. Photography has also been an area of exploration, leading to work involving 3D images and cyanotypes.

Since graduating Elise has been offered an artist residency at Bath Artists' Studios, which will culminate in putting on an exhibition in their gallery space and giving a talk. Even though Elise is in the early stages of research, she is already inspired to explore how history, architecture and tourism come together in Bath today.

Elise Menghini lives and works in Bath.

# Kelly Munro

**2013 BA Silversmithing and Jewellery,** Edinburgh College of Art.

Kelly Munro's inspiration is drawn from her heritage and homeland. Kelly was born in a small town in the far north coast of Scotland, well known for its historical fishing industry. Being surrounded by small abandoned ports around the coast, has given Kelly a particular interest in fishing equipment used in the past and present. This inspiration is reflected in the lobster pots as a starting point for her graduation show work. This has evolved through stages of material exploration and settled at the combination of 'weathering' wood and traditional metal techniques.

The technique of intricate saw piercing enables Kelly to create nets and lightweight structures. Her aim is to shadow the forms of the nets and pots, and loosely interoperate these shapes in her own way. The technique of pyrography plays an important role in the pieces allowing her to create often detailed patterns combined with charred edges and loose paint strokes, mirroring the intricately knotted nets of the trade combined with wind beaten driftwood. Kelly's work aims to portray the rustic look of items found near harbours and tide lines.

Kelly Munro lives and works in Edinburgh.

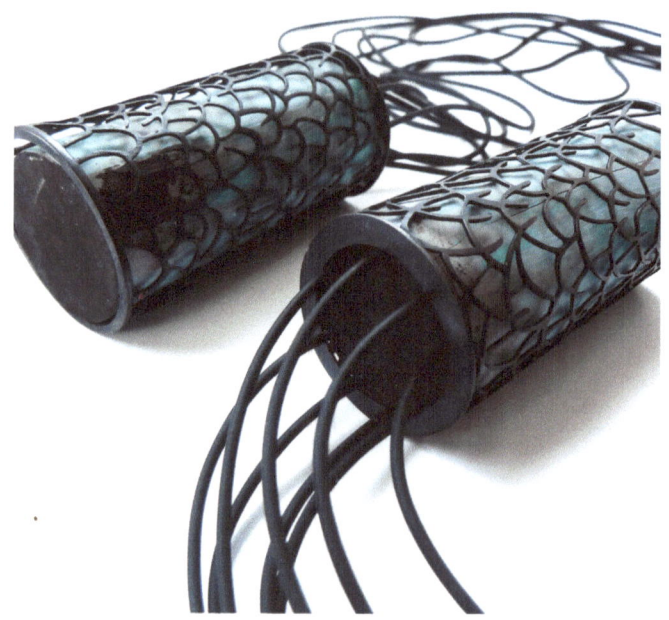

*Barrel Neckalce* 2013
Mixed media

# Izzy Parker

**2013 MA Goldsmithing,** Silversmithing, Metalwork and Jewellery, Royal College of Art.
**2007 BA Three Dimensional Design Materials and Critical Practice,** Camberwell College of Arts.

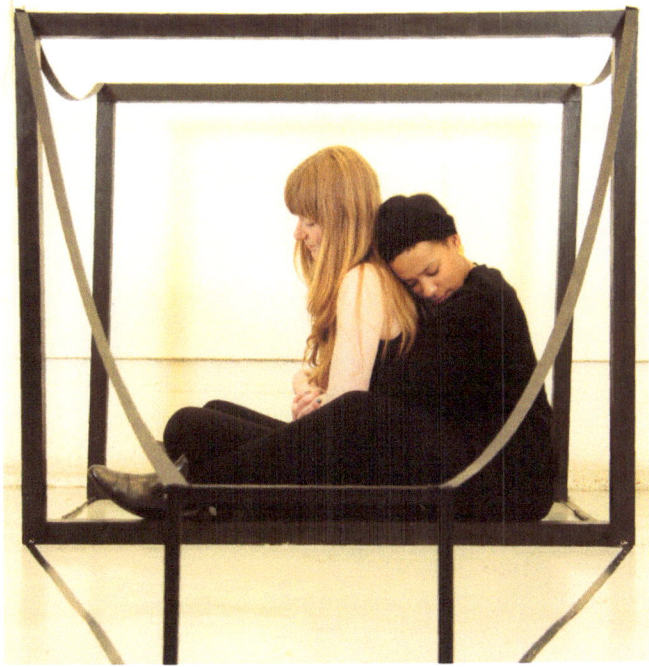

*Intimacy Frame*
Pine, steel
Photographer Adele Watts

Izzy Parker is running a live interactive experiment for the touring exhibition as an extension to her most recent body of work *Intimacy* series. The series contains a number of research elements that include participatory experimentation with environments, objects and jewellery that explore cultural anthropology, each element exploring and questioning our perspectives on social boundaries.

Izzy will perform at the private views of each venue. Launching at the New Ashgate Gallery during *The Intimate Act of Jewellery* she asks participants to join her with the restriction of no spoken dialogue; her jewellery will direct the interaction, challenging personal space boundaries. Can jewellery provoke physical contact between two strangers?

Izzy Parker lives and works in London.

# Anastasija Pjatnicka

**2014 MA Jewellery Design,** Manchester School of Art.
**2013 BA Product Design (ceramics),** Limerick School of Art and Design.

With ceramics being Anastasiji Pjatnicka's main medium, she believes that it is somewhat underrated in jewellery. It is indeed a stiff, relatively fragile and heavy material, but by incorporating mixed media most problems can be solved, and the shape, texture and colour possibilities are truly spectacular.

After all, jewellery is not just about function.

This collection of statement neckpieces happened by bringing together armour, animal skins and geometric abstractions. Looking into mechanics of birds' wing was particularly inspiring.

The pieces are made from individually hand-built ceramic segments that are bound together by a thread or attached to the fabric base. Such a construction enables a good fit to the body and makes them comfortable to wear. As one of the focuses of work is the surfaces that can be achieved in ceramics, the titles refer to the names of the glazes used.

Anastasija's takes great pleasure in making pieces of art that are meant not just for display, but also for interaction, even if it is not on everyday basis. For her, directly engaging with a skilfully and creatively made piece and learning to recognize and value that skill and creativity is what craft is all about.

Anastasija Pjatnicka lives and works in Manchester.

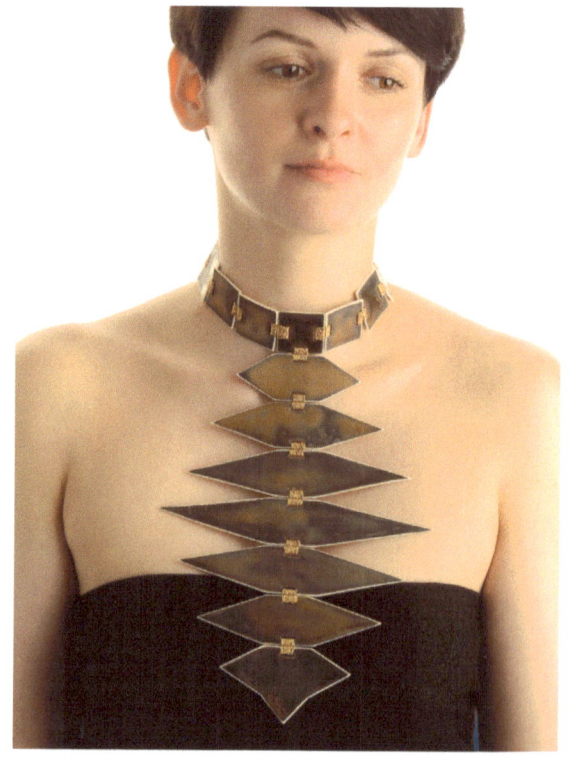

*Bronze*
Glazed porcelain and polyester

# Hajnalka Rezes

**2014 MA Ceramics**, University for the Creative Arts, Farnham.

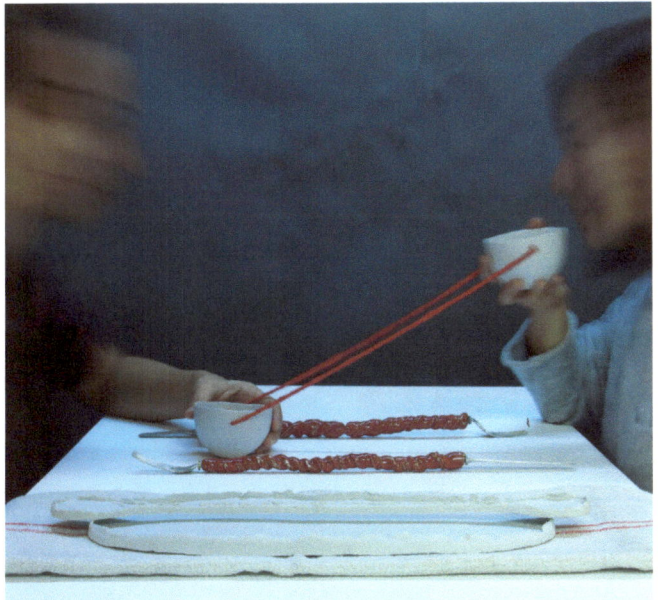

*Red connected cutlery*
Connected bowls, double ended spoons with a plate

Hajnalka Rezes makes interactive objects that not only represent the emotional connection between people but also generates it. She is looking for empathy because it is often recognized that this is the phenomenon that connects otherwise isolated individuals. It is also a very basis of all human interaction.

As traditional cutlery renders the ancient and intimate act of sharing food physically and symbolically more distant, these interactive utensils help to process emotional information and manage emotional dynamics.

Hajnalka Rezes lives and works in Surrey.

# Charlotte Stockley

**2013 BA Three Dimensional Design (ceramics),** University for the Creative Arts, Farnham.

Charlotte Stockley designs thrown porcelain tableware. After the porcelain is thrown on the wheel it is altered both immediately and at later stages. This process gives a dynamic look and ensures that every piece is unique. Porcelain is a tactile material, which translates through when handling the finished objects.

Charlotte's inspiration originated partly from growing fruit and vegetables on her allotment garden but also the shapes of the many insects found in conjunction within this environment. The grooves and dimples found on the tableware are translations of three dimensional surface and pattern from this rich design source. There is a fusion of ideas which emulates many of the mixed styles of ingredients used in cooking. One particular influence is the Mediterranean recipes and ethos of Yotam Ottolenghi who describes his cuisine in reference to vibrant, daring colours. Charlotte's drawings, made into transfers and fired on to the ware, also draw on influences from 1950s surface pattern and tableware.

Charlotte Stockley lives and works in Surrey.

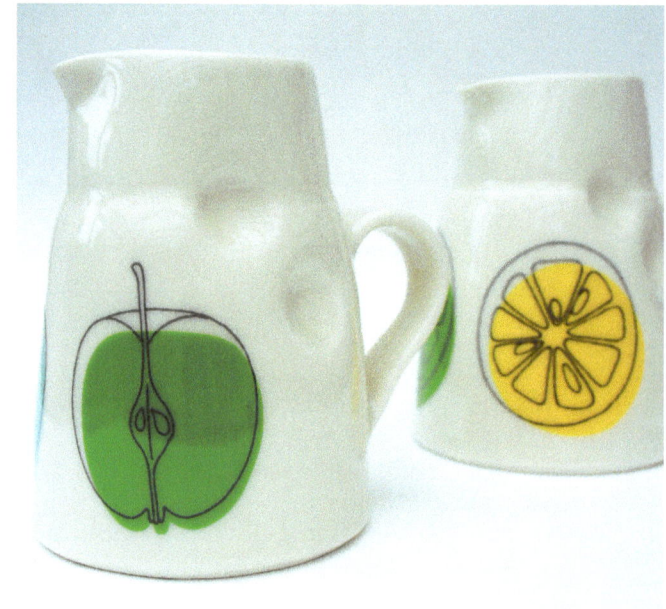

*Apples and lemons and limes*
Porcelain jugs

43

# Julia Webster

**2013 MA Contemporary Crafts (glass),** University for the Creative Arts, Farnham.
**1982 BA 3DD,** West Surrey College of Art and Design.

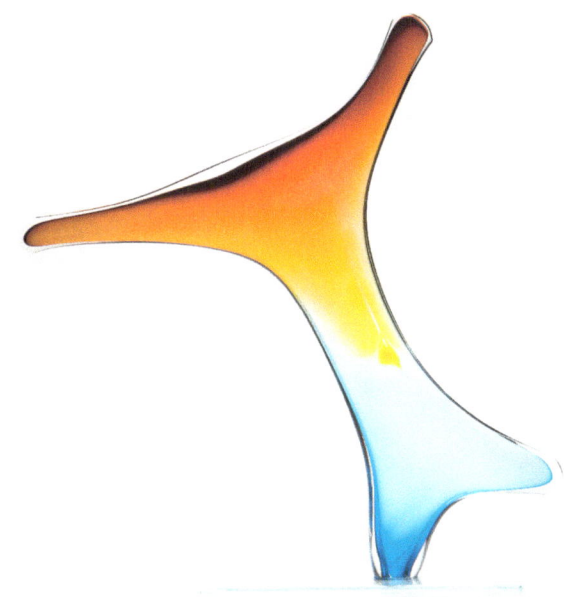

*Tilt*
Glass

Julia Webster creates work predominantly in glass as an expressive medium to explore the real, the poetic and the multi-sensory qualities of balance, flow, void, mass and movement in stillness. The artist has a range of influences, including dance, music, travel, mythology and notions of the unending journey of the earth, turning on its axis through space and time. Julia's starting points include flowing gestural characters generated via brush calligraphy. She combines this with figurative drawing and dance photography. Experimentation plays a significant role in ideas development guided by visual imagination and materials.

Julia embraces a variety of processes including mould making, hot glass blowing and centrifuging, kiln casting and fusing. Exploring a variety of qualities in glass such as flow properties, tonal and colour saturation, density, refraction and reflection. In some cases forms are cut to create edges that offer points of transition and tension between inside and outside surfaces and opportunities for playing with balance points.

Julia Webster lives and works in Surrey.

# Penny Wheeler

**2012 MA Textiles**, Bath Spa University.
**2009 BA Fashion and Textiles**, Bath Spa University.

Penny Wheeler is an accomplished technician whose work embraces the complexities of the craft. Extending the possibilities of the grid which defines weave – Penny subverts the conventions of the discipline by extending the possibilities of the loom. Fascinated by the construction of weave and its potential Penny's work explores the irregular in the regular and communicates the essential relationship between fibres, yarns and the frame. Penny's particular interest is landscape; the colour and forms within it, our reactions to it, and the processes that change it. Technique and concept are bought together to communicate both the surface and what is hidden beneath.

Penny Wheeler lives and works in Bath.

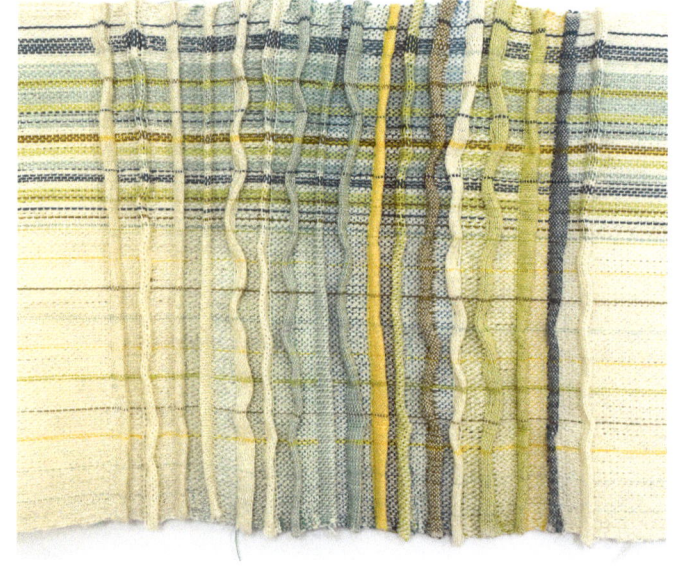

*Pleat Investigations 1*
Paper, silk

# Hannah Rose Whittle

**2013 BA Three Dimensional Materials Practice,** University of Brighton.

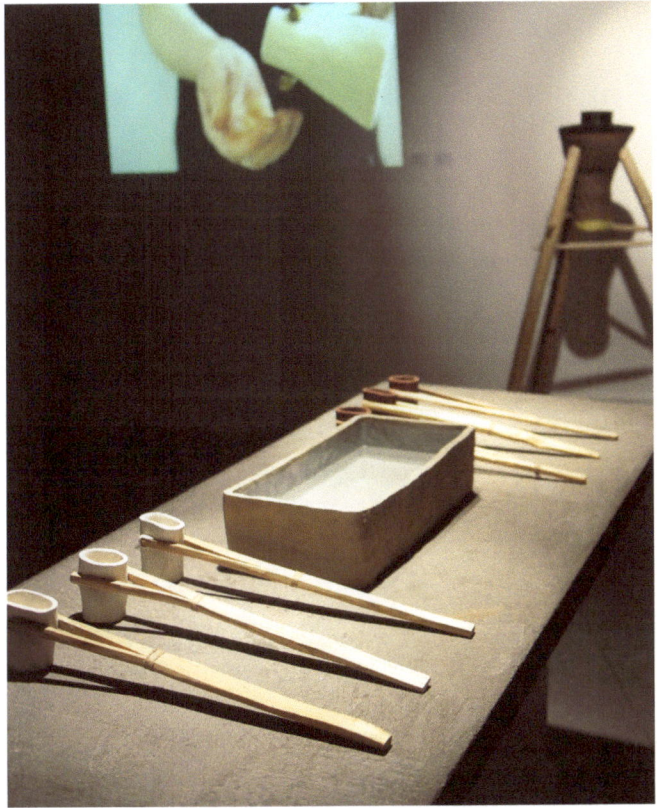

From the series *'Implements for Cleansing Rituals'* installation view
Video projection, Unfired porcelain and black clay, green wood,
twine, reduction fired ceramic

Hannah Rose Whittle's practice is heavily influenced by her scholarship to study fine art ceramics in Japan, followed by her return to continue studies in the West. Through an intimate engagement with materials, Hannah's work is an exploration into the notion of transience and impermanence. With an interest in the direct experience of time passing in an age of a fast paced, constantly moving society, her work questions - can time be made tangible?

Hannah has developed her practice through the ritual of making. Combining slow and methodical with energetic and immediate action, gives her work a sense of tension and chance. Hannah is interested in the relevance of water as innate in clay and wood, how they are wet together and become dry together. Through a series of green wood and clay vessels she explores the initial intimate relationship between these materials by creating tools for cleansing rituals and time keeping devices.

Through experimenting with wood ash to create traditional glazes, and including industrial colour, the forms take on a dynamic aesthetic with an emphasis on the interplay between wood and clay.

Hannah Rose Whittle lives and works in Essex.

# Simon Wilks

**2013 BA Three Dimensional Design,** University of Wolverhampton.
**2015 MA Ceramic Design,** Staffordshire University.

Simon Wilks' work explores the relationships between ceramic design and craft. Using Japanese tableware as an inspiration, he combines slip cast with hand thrown vessels; placing rustic with controlled form and shape. The slip cast and hand thrown vessels are situated upon beautifully treated wood; either polished mahogany, laminated plywood or burnt oak. Further contrasts are sort with rustic textured slab platters fired and hand crafted spoons, spatulas and scoops to echo the natural qualities in both the clay and wood.

Tableware affords Simon a particular sublime experience undertaken when dining, those moments of time in which we are able to indulge in the combined experience of refined food and design.

Simon Wilkes lives and works in Shropshire.

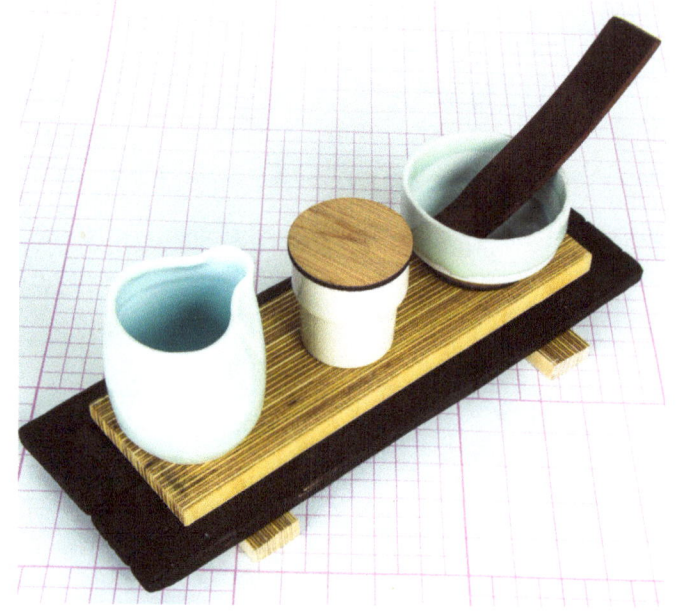

*Tableware 15*
Hand thrown porcelain sauce jug, slip cast bowl and vessel with lid, mahogany spatula presented on a burnt oak and laminated stand

47

# Cristina Zani

**2012 MA Jewellery,** Edinburgh College of Art.

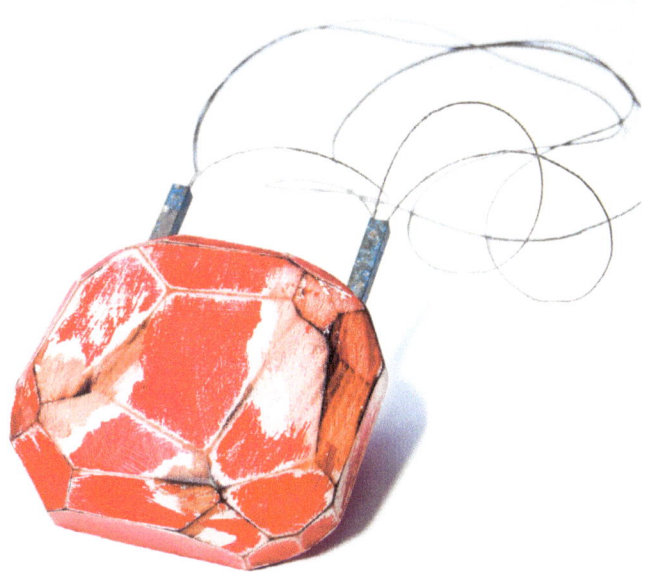

*My Seoul*
Red pendant, wood, patinated brass, acrylic paint, linen thread,

Inspired by Italo Calvino's *Invisible Cities*, Cristina Zani's collection is a reflection on the urban environment and the concept of invisibility. The series *My Seoul* is influenced by the contrasting architecture of South Korea.

The choice and juxtaposition of materials, shapes and colours echoes its landscape: sombre modern buildings intertwined with colourful and ancient wooden temples and palaces. Like those buildings, her pieces show the vulnerability of wood and metal when exposed to time and elements; the layers and colours that slowly transform with the passing of years. They are simple in form, but rich in stories and complexities.

Cristina says: "Underpinned by my fascination with literature, semiotics, travel, architecture, colours, textures and materials, my work is the tangible testimonial of my journey through cities."

Cristina Zani lives and works in the Lake District.

# Sevak Zargarian

**2013 BA Ceramic Design,** Central St Martins.

Sevak Zargarian has a passion for material exploration, ignited on a foundation course where he experimented with copper rods and porcelain paperclay, witnessing the transformative powers of the kiln. Sevak has since kept a focus on process, with influences from studio pottery and the different techniques available, and the tactile qualities of clay.

For this collection, Sevak used grog (fired ceramic pieces) as the craft element in his exploration of the liminal space between craft and design. Making this the central focus of the project, he has experimented with different making techniques and finishes, to create vessels which are unique, as the grog is randomly placed through the reverse casting process. The surface is then sponged and sanded away to reveal the grog beneath the surface.

Sevak Zargarian lives and works in London.

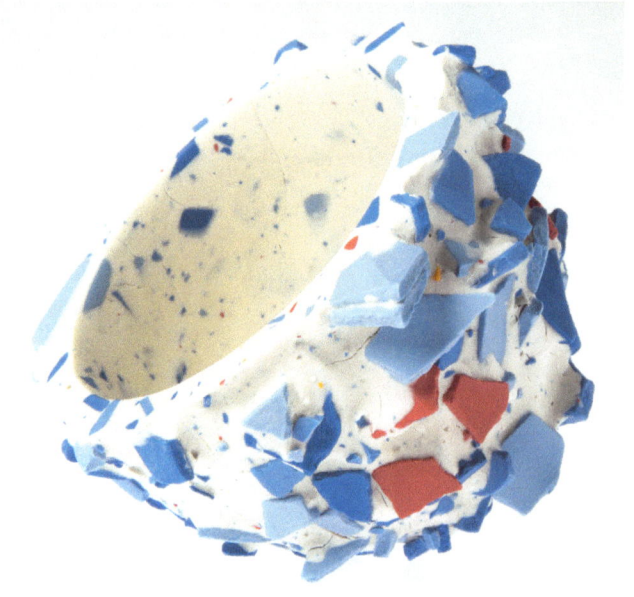

*Se'Grogged Bowl (BlueRed)*
Porcelain

www.ingramcontent.com/pod-product-compliance
Lightning Source LLC
Chambersburg PA
CBHW051058180526
45172CB00002B/691